Deck of Poetry

The Wolf's Ink

𝔇𝔢𝔠𝔨 𝔬𝔣 𝔓𝔬𝔢𝔱𝔯𝔶

The Wolf's Ink

S.Grewal

Deck of Poetry: The Wolf's Ink

Copyright © 2024 S.Grewal

All rights reserved. No part of this book may be reproduced, distributed, or transmitted in any form without the prior written permission of the publisher, except in the case of brief quotations in the context of book reviews.

For permission requests, write to the publisher, addressed at deckofpoetry@gmail.com

ISBN: 978-1-7382785-0-3 (Paperback)

First Paperback Edition February 2024.

@deckofpoetry
www.deckofpoetry.com

DEDICATION

*This book is dedicated
to those tired of the shores
and are finally looking
to swim in the deep end.*

Disclaimer: No Artificial Intelligence (AI) was used in the composition of these poetic cards and their context.

LEGEND

The Ace of Spade represents the Deck of Poetry symbolically. Every poem falls into one of the three categories below.

Clovers represent inspiration and truth poems.

Hearts represent love and romance poems.

Diamonds represent wordplay and haikus.

CONTENTS

Preface ix

Clovers - Inspiration and Truth

I - Land of the Inspired 1
II - Her Awakening.. 29
III - Seekers of Truth... 39
IV - Dark Society 69

Hearts – Love and Romance

I - Howls of Romance 85
II - Earthly Love... 111

Diamonds – Wordplay and Haikus

I - Dancing in Ink 141
II - Word-Smith & Play.. 169
III - Haiku Den 187

PREFACE

Symbolic across cultures, meet the Wolf who joins you on this journey through the poetic spectrum. As you begin this adventure together, the Wolf is intertwined within the poetic cards to guide you spiritually with intuition, instinct, independence, and freedom. This journey will provide you with context, insight, revelations, or illustrations that will accompany each poetic card.

You begin at sunrise in the **Land of the Inspired**. From there, your broadened horizons leave you destined to become **Seekers of Truth** to better grapple with the inner workings of human nature. Upon nightfall, your **Howls of Romance** echo in the horizon for love. As the clock strikes midnight, creativity consumes your desire to express and unfold. Thus, under the moonlit sky, you begin **Dancing in Ink**, playing with words as you ultimately reach the **Haiku Den** to end the night.

Mirroring life itself, this journey holds diverse aspects that will define your essence. You are made up of numerous facets that collectively form the entirety of who you are. Venture mindfully down this path as you gather poetic cards along the way. This journey was written for you.

Land of the Inspired

Part I

Live your life without limits because sometimes the sky isn't even high enough. The only limits that exist are the ones forged by your state of mind. Change your perspective, tilt the angle, rewrite the script and life will make its way.

LIMITLESS

How can the
sky be the limit
when we have footprints
on the moon?
Even outer space
cannot limit
a mind which is in tune.

The world has so much to explore, and so does the world within you. Every day we can improve ourselves and be more in tune with who we are. Exploring our depths is key to becoming the better version of ourselves. Venturing out to the unseen places inside us will enrich aspects of our character.

Think about how you've discovered some of your passions or hobbies in life. You had to experiment to find a chord that struck within you. Imagine if you never took a shot at your passion and lived your entire life never knowing what you can love so damn much. Finding out what you love, hate, are good (and bad) at will always bring you closer to your true self.

TRUE-SELF

Explore all the
hidden and forbidden
islands within you.
Become your true self
and the world will have
no other choice
but to know the real you.

The heart and mind are two different animals. One is wild and one is far more calculated. The heart is never meant to be caged, for it thrives in the wild. This is how it finds opportunities that the mind cannot always foresee. Sometimes you love things you cannot explain. You can safeguard and lock up the heart, but it will never relish the same life experiences and highs or lows of a wild heart.

HEARTS

A logical heart
will never experience
    the richness
    the sharpness
    the deepness
    the beat miss
experienced by
a wild heart.

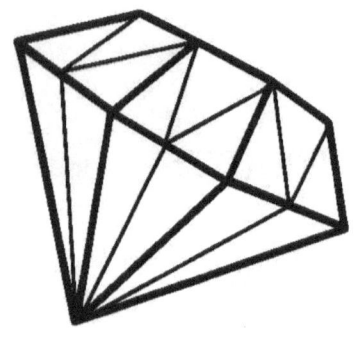

Stay resilient as a diamond in a world full of pressure.

DIAMOND

Diamond hearted
and minded.
Cannot be
easily broken
nor founded.

Life can sway
in the left way
yet I will replenish
continuously
as a fountain.

Growth is an endless ladder; every day we can sculpt ourselves and continue to evolve. Never let that fire inside of you die. Let it be the True North to your life's compass.

GROWTH

Diamonds inside my veins
the fire rushes forever.

Like a bird flying in the rain
I soar through the downfalls
of life's uncanny weather.

Plant seeds inside my pain
let them blossom out...
growth is the endeavor.

Diamonds inside my veins
resilient under pressure.

Land of the Inspired

The most beautiful thing about our mind is perspective. The ability to shift perspective can simply change the color, shape and understanding of our world. I'm sure we all have made mistakes in our life that we suddenly regret as we start backtracking on how things could've been different if we did this or that. This cycle is only helpful if the train is taken one way to learn instead of getting stuck going back and forth in our powerless past. Find the silver lining in every mistake and view them as an opportunity.

REGRETS

There are no regrets
in this world.
Every mistake
is a hidden lesson,
another undiscovered
ocean pearl.

In a world full of overwhelming opinions, you must always find your axis. Never let the world dictate your worth. Time and experience are all we have, and our life is the price.

PRICELESS

World full of prices,
yet you are so priceless.
Like everything else
that fades away
on this earth,
money cannot capture
your life's essence,
your endangered worth.

This poetic card is an ode to all artists and creators. Are we solely the creators, or does art itself in a way create who we are too? I believe on a deeper subconscious level it is also creating us. Symbiosis.

ARTIST-PARADOX

I do not only write these poems,
they also write me.
The designer being
simultaneously designed.

I am finite within ticking time
yet in this quantum paradox
my art lets me press rewind.

It's an intricate intertwine
between the artist soul
and the magnetic destiny
of the art to which one binds.

*So, ask yourself, are you truly living?
Just like the prism reflects the spectrum
of light, so should you reflect yours.*

LIVING

The ocean on this earth
is the water inside of me.
For its various dimensions
mirror my simple complexity.
Still today as the monk.
Flow tomorrow as the magician.
I create aggressive waves
to wash away all that is within.
For without any of these traits
I truly would not be living.

As we grow wise, we tend to see our close circle become smaller. Life experiences, age, or both, give us clarity and inevitably a more concentrated life. I've always been one for quality over quantity, especially in my social world.

I'd rather have an army of three I can trust inside out than roam with many who have ulterior motives. Double-down on the value you place on those who stay by your side no matter what.

Life is short, and the circle gets shorter.

RESIDUAL

Spiritual individual.
Evolving my third-eye
is a continual ritual
to elevate the visual.
Seeing right through you
is habitually instinctual.
Separating friend from foe,
I strictly value the residual.

Land of the Inspired

Sharpened double-edged sword moving through this world with no regrets...staying loyal as a wolf in a pack, yet dangerous to any threat like a jungle lion on the attack.

DOUBLE-EDGED

Become the sharpest
double-edged sword.
Be known as
the greatest friend
one can ever have
yet also the most
dangerous enemy
one would never want.

Land of the Inspired

BLACKSMITH

Sharpen your mind
with the same intent
a superior blacksmith
would sharpen
the mighty sword
for his beloved King
in the dark mist
of the greatest war.

Life's most precious experiences are made up of moments where chemistry is at its peak. Now, if you think chemistry refers to only love, you are wrong. Chemistry is created with any person; whether it's a lover, stranger, friend or family member. Surrounding yourself with the right people is one of the most powerful things you can do to better yourself.

I think it is important for us to sometimes sit back, fall into third person perspective and start observing the type of influence we associate ourselves with. Sometimes, you don't even notice the negative energy others may radiate.

CHEMISTRY

I seek the type of
chemistry
where the only sign
is never enough time.

Her Awakening

Part II

Interesting fact, the hummingbird is the only bird that can truly hover. It can fly straight up, down or backwards and forwards.

EAGLE EYE

She had an eagle eye
for all his lethal lies.
Backwards he'd glide
as the hummingbird
without knowing...
she had already planned
for his coming demise.

Sometimes the world fails you. The cards don't always line up in your favor every single day. Find yourself a passion or a hobby that lights your inner fuse and gives you a mental haven. Our minds are so powerful. They are an ever absorbing and evolving mechanism. Some may find their peace and joy in reading or writing books whereas others find it in music. Everyone needs something. What is your thing?

BLUE ROSE

Knowing the world
could never save her,
she found security
in words of meaning
to slay her demons.
Building herself castles
with sharpened swords,
she's that rare blue rose
with a thousand thorns.

An ode to women that know themselves and never bend for the eye of society. In this poetic card I capture the mystic symbolism of the lotus flower to represent the resilience and strength of women. Flowers are commonly used to portray the beauty of a woman; thus, I chose to bring light to a different attribute – resilience.

To be resilient is to know oneself. By knowing oneself, one knows how to thrive or adapt in any climate; whether it's the best of days or the darkest. The lotus is beautiful and unique as it grows in the mud, submerges underwater at night and emerges during the day, sparklingly clean. In many cultures, this process is associated with spirituality and rebirth.

LOTUS

She truly knows herself
like a resilient
lotus flower
fully conscious
of the sun's power
and how to thrive
in times of no shine
during every dark hour.

Her Awakening

BUTTERFLY

You only have one life.
Let your prism reflect
all its beautiful colors.
Don't suppress those
soulful inner covers
of your true being.
Break out of the cocoon,
let your butterfly free...
and rain down abundance
like a thousand monsoons.

Seekers of Truth

Part III

Always stay true to yourself. The last thing you would want to do is become a reflection of other people's perception.

IMPRESSIONS

You cannot impress
the entire world...
as it was never
made to be won.

It is in our human nature to judge, compare and reflect. We live in a digital age where the lens is amplified on everyone. We continuously flow through a stream of information on how to be and/or where we fall on this spectrum. The reality is there will always be opposing sides and different opinions. Never should we fall victim to these inevitabilities at the expense of who we are.

MORALS

What a contradictory world
we all live in.
People strongly judge
those who are too different
yet undervalue those too similar.
Moral of the story is
always be yourself
it is the only thing
you'll truly ever own.

We all have a core inside. It is magnetic, and grounds us as human beings. When we stray away from our core, life seems to be out of flow, and things never fall in the right place. With this comes self-realization and alignment, which eventually makes the world fall into place like pieces to a puzzle.

CORE

We all have a core
just like the Earth
to which we are
magnetically prone too.
This core defines us
foundationally...
just like a tree's roots.
While our branches grow
a million different types
of leaves and fruits.

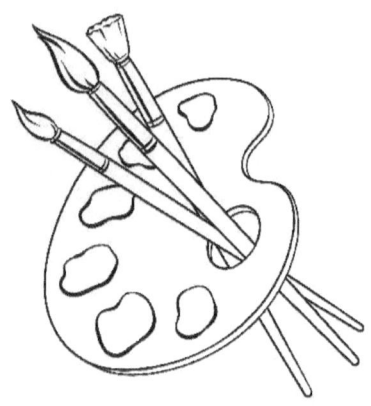

Being open-minded can enrich one's life in many ways. Sometimes your set of colors is limiting, whereas the world has an endless array of options.

Explore the world to learn about yourself, and in return the world explores you.

CANVAS

Most people maneuver
around the world covered
with self-painted colors.
It's far more beautiful and rich
to roam with an empty canvas
and let the world be your artist.

It all begins within; character over everything. Appearance may give initial impressions, but being a gentleman will always start from the inside out. In other words, you cannot buy it, rather only live it.

GENTLEMAN

Beyond the physical elegance
of classy suits,
watches and boots,
a gentleman
in the truest sense
is embodied
only through character
traceable by the
sprout of one's roots.

If you are alive and conscious; you are forever as that is all you know. Never forget you are the main character of your story. It begins and ends with you.

FOREVER

Never ever
lose yourself
in the midst
of chasing
someone else.
They may only be
temporary...
but you are yourself,
you are forever.

VASES

Fill your life's vase
with many flowers
of your soul and self.

The emptier the vase,
the more it'll attract unwanted people
to manipulate the strings of your life.

Good things in life
require no extra space,
they become a part of you.

As the world becomes more materialistic, we tend to forget our souls are fueled by energy that begins within. Building ourselves from the inside out should always take priority over the ever-changing ways we tend to fill these voids with materialism. Feeling good about yourself begins with you, and only then expressing it is worthwhile.

Materialistic trends are always being replaced. We find ourselves looking forward to the next big thing as the ones we own become irrelevant. However, there's nothing wrong with loving nice things when your priorities are in order.

DESIGNER

So many are focused
on chasing the latest
designer brands...
forgetting to ever truly
design themselves
from the inside out.

In a digital world where information or new ideas go viral and become widely accepted, we become surrounded by emerging trends that continue to replace one another. At times, they evoke such a strong pull, urging us to either hop on board or risk being left behind.

In certain instances, new trends are good and align with who we are. However, it is a great loss when we decide to dull away our sharp edges that make us individually unique for the sake of fitting in.

TRENDS

Don't blindly
just follow trends
and lose your very edges
in a world full of pretend.
Every time you do,
your character blends
as it starts to become
more and more shallow
...a hollow den.

In this poetic card I look to capture the essence of karma. It was challenging, especially because I wanted to approach it differently from the usual cliché that we are all numb too. The term mind-state is often used but I believe the essence of karma lies within the heart, hence heart-state.

KARMA

An eye for an eye
or a bridge for a bridge.
Will you let the water under
or flow over like sin?
I prefer humanity
we are all kin.
Come full circle...
living in the aroma
of good karma
is the heart-state
in which we all win.

EYES

Is it true or a lie?
Word to the wise...
the answer lies
in the subtle
signature
of one's eyes.

Be careful of false hopes, some people may never change. We certainly should be aware of those with bad intentions.

P.S. Snakes, as in the animals, are fascinating creatures of our beautiful planet. This is strictly metaphorical.

SNAKE

You cannot change
the true core of a person.
Some cores are magnetic,
others are repellent.
Be vigilant of those
carrying venom
disguised as honey.
A snake can shed its skin
all life long...
yet it will still be a snake.

It's truly remarkable the way people change who they are and how they act if they are to be anonymous. You don't believe me? Well, social media is perhaps the biggest proof; think about the things being said by those who hide behind an alias account.

This poetic card isn't solely about that, but rather the human phenomenon of how some people would only truly be themselves if they were hidden - whether good or bad. For some, being mysterious allows them to express their creative sides more freely.

TRUE COLORS

Lend most
a mask
to disguise
their past
and watch
as they
begin...
to paint
all their
true colors.

The truth is like an answer to a known math question. There is no room for error. Seeking and speaking the truth is the highest pursuit for us all. In today's world, with so much false information being spread, it is more important than ever. None of us are perfect, but knowing what to strive for and actively doing so can be collectively enough.

TRUTH

They say many hate
when I speak the truth
with the skin peeled off.

I tell them to never worry
and it will never phase me
since we all know
their sugar dissolves.

The truth about truth is
it wears no sly coat.
By swimming in the sea
of transparency
is how we all evolve.

Dark Society

Part IV

GLASS OF MIND

Fragile minds
hidden beneath
the body's physical design
shall forever remain
shatterable...
like a glass of wine.

Dark Society

In the hierarchy of life, may we never lose sight of what makes us human. This poetic card is a worldly reflection of this desire to be consumers and consumed. This takes place to the point we become blind to our true nature, closing off all the valves that make us unique and free.

It's not focused on delving into economics or critiquing capitalism; that would be a separate discussion. Instead, the aim is to shine light on one of the side effects that ensnare many individuals. It is, nevertheless, feasible to thrive within a capitalist society by retaining our originality and avoiding the tendency to mindlessly overconsume.

SHAPELESS

This capitalism
m a t r i x
tends to focus
most minds
only on the basics.
Consuming all space
for ordinary thought
and our long-lost art
of being shapeless.

Dark Society

This poetic card is a wakeup call to the realities of our society and what is truly important. It builds upon the 'Shapeless' poetic card. We have forgotten our ways of connection. Questions we must ask ourselves such as what is truly fulfilling, and food for our souls? What makes us human?

The answer is and always has been purpose, love, growth, connection, family, community, passion and art. These fundamental aspects stand in stark contrast to the allure of material possessions, many bound for obsolescence from their inception.

CONSUMERISM

Blinded by lights,
highlight social media
and screens full of hysteria.
Consumerism consuming
away at unguarded souls
taking a grand toll
with shallow promises
of it's yours, it's sold!

There is no one left
to tell the truth no more.
Inner visions are blurry
envisioning a hurry
to materialistic flurries
that might make one feel
their life is finally worthy.
Worthy...of the unworthy.

Being a rebel is not always a bad thing; sometimes it is the best way to create change for the better. Think of influential figures of history such as Socrates, Martin Luther King Jr., Malala Yousafzai, or the rebellious women who fought for voting rights. Let us rebel when chasing for the greater good.

REBEL

Society tends to
paint all rebels
in a negative light.
Yet the rebel mind
has been responsible
for all great changes;
both good and bad.
Rebels bring chaos
to balance order.

Dark Society

This poetic card is about love, unity, and keeping our moral compass intact no matter the storm. The world had many dark moments in the past, has dark moments today, and will inevitably have dark moments to come. Seeking the truth and spreading light is higher living. In the end, the message will always be the same - never lose sight of the light.

BEACON

The world is far too upside down.
Blurry lines between tyrant and crown.
Gravity weighing down the conscience.
Collective hives under false pretense.

Every hero is deemed the villain
before they can even clean sins.
Who are you and I to even reason?
Black Hole mentality swallows whole
the very scarce fabrics of sanity.
Ignorance is the new desired canopy.

Can you see with eyes wide open?
It's us, truth magnets full of might
sending out beacons of God's light
in hopes to shift the worldly axis right.

Dark Society

Take a moment to think about what makes your heart move, happy, loved, or safe? Now, tell me why every other heart wouldn't need the same? This poetic card came to me in the dark times of our world.

It pushed me to look beyond and capture the roots behind every dark period the world experiences. The underlying foundations of unity versus division, misguided beliefs, power, zero-sum games, and simply being numb to what's humane are some of the major roots I stumbled upon.

STRINGS

Broken hearts cry music,
only the silence is listening.
World divides further apart
as if earthquakes shatter apart
our threads of unity as humans.

The only difference between
you, me, and all of them is sold
illusions masked in confusion.

Love, the timeless healer of all,
potion that seals and dissolves
a long forgotten sacred solution.

Look inside, move your heartstrings
and tell me why every other heart
won't need the same movement?

Dark Society

DIVINE VEINS

For they shower the truth
with the devil's dark rain
to flood out any light
not knowing it's in vain.

For we have resilient aims
illuminating our wicked pain,
diamond hearts and divine veins.

Flowers blooming in concrete jungles
lovers of life and all it claims...
as we venture out into the abyss,
sacrificing for our righteous reigns.

Howls of Romance

Part I

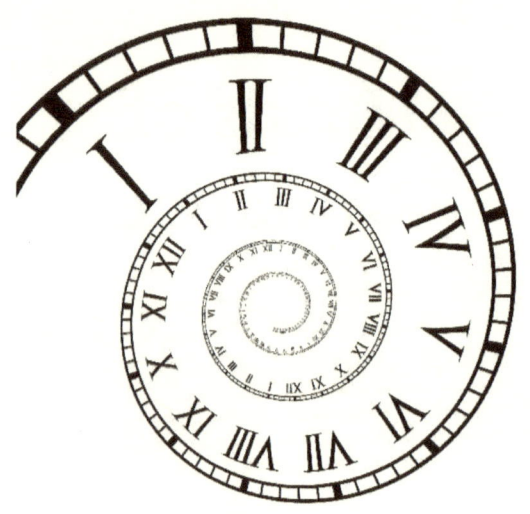

TIMELESS

She roams
around the world
so timeless...
everything about her
makes the time disappear.

All she knows is herself. Society cannot chain her, for she is chainless.

SHE'S WILD

She is so damn wild.
Flower through concrete.
Lucid dreams without sleep.
Dopamine rushes yet she's so clean.
Lives freely outside the world's seams.
Never bends for any man's keep.
Never pretends, she ascends...
She is soul-deep.

HER ZEAL

Her entire being
is a zeal for the divine.
Way she's put together
from her inquisitive mind
to her beating drum heart,
she only lives in rhymes.

From her head to her toes
to elegant curvature lines...
her soul is connected by grace
covered in an exquisite vine.

Dopamine inducing...
heroine seducing...
five words producing...
"will she ever be mine?"

Have you ever come across someone that makes you lose all sense of time and worry? Rather, have you ever come across a piece of a puzzle that fits so perfectly? Well, the highest of these charms will make you content with life's inevitable death.

CHARM

My charm radiates deep
as the ocean's depth.
Every move I make
inhales her breath.
Slowly casting away
all her fears from
life's inevitable death.

Capturing the romantic balance between opposing sides, one remains grounded while the other stays elevated; Yin and Yang. One seeks beyond the horizon, looking for dangerous truths and adventure. The other builds an anchor ashore, a fortified castle one calls home.

ECSTASY

My free spirit
pushes her mind
into the unknown,
exploring the far corners
of her mental complexity.
The pendulum swings
from third-eye views
of the pharaohs
to sacred grounded
stones of density.
She knows routine
but I know ecstasy.

HIEROGLYPHICS

We always push to the edge
adventuring out into the abyss.
The chemistry is swift.
Witness moving mountains
the way our auras come together
and spill over like mist.
Mythical love...
inscribed in hieroglyphs.
This love story is exactly
what we were once told
could never exist.

This poetic card is for those who experience cerebral love - that serene moment in which you both vibrate at the same frequency to deep dive into one another's minds to surf the same tides.

ORIGAMI

We surf on
intellectual waves
and vibrate
the same frequency.
Cerebral foreplay
keeps us high as tsunamis
yet we never drown
as our geometric bond
takes shape of origami.

*She is the type to give life to life,
to make you feel like you've already lived twice,
the type that just can no longer be typed...*

FLOWER

She's the type
that can touch
a flower
and leave it filled
with immortality.

DARK ANGEL

An angel comfortable
with the darkness.
Her plot twist
leaves my mind
on a sharp drift.
My crime is searching
for a sign so divine
where time may ever let
our two souls align.

She is shapeless and flows as freely as the ocean itself. Limitless in her existence the world cannot come to define her, for she leaves her essence wherever she goes. Her elusive manner keeps the world on its toes.

SHE MOVES

She's moves as if
the ocean in swift motion.
She moves as if
the world does not see her.
She moves as if
society cannot teach her.
She moves as if
the ground is not beneath her.
She moves, she moves
spreading her contagious ether.

PARANORMAL

She's a living
Goddess
amongst us
mere mortals.
Her every smile
opens portals
that will leave you
curiously stuck inside
the paranormal.

MY MUSE

She's my muse.
Violin strings singing out the blues.
She's my muse. Her red dress infused
with red wine hues as her pheromones
suffocate my senses, I forget all I knew.

She's my muse. Wounded alpha wolf
howling out his love for the moon.
She's my muse. Hourglass of time
her love rains down shrines of monsoons.
She's my muse.

Earthly Love

Part II

Earthly Love

SUNRISE

Something about her
keeps me replenished
every single day.
She's like an endless
stream of water
flowing as the rivers,
or like the kissing Sun
she presents herself daily
and yet is still needed
for life tomorrow.

Earthly Love

Have you ever crossed paths with a mind so profound that the conversation took you down an avenue never foreseen? To the point where you begin unlocking ideas and realizations you would never tap into without the other person. There is but magic in the dialectical exchange between two minds. Some of the greatest ideas known in the world today have come about this way.

CONVERSATIONS

Scenic conversations.
Who would've guessed
that a dance between
two synchronized voices
could become so raw
and adventurous.
Tapping into many
undiscovered places,
the chemistry of our minds
can build up an oasis.

Earthly Love

Let me come visit...I'll cut through the clutter and shine a new light on our existence.

Let me come visit...I'll leave your mind feeling weightless before the day's end.

GRAPEVINES

Why don't you come
and tell me...
what is going on inside
that beautiful mind?
Let me come visit
and cut through
all of those grapevines.

Earthly Love

Sun and Moon.
Day and Night.
Yin and Yang.
Left for every Right.
Darkness inside the Light.
Eyes for every Sight.

BONNIE & CLYDE

She is the
holster to my pistol,
sheath for my sword,
ice for all my fire,
ink inside my words.
As Bonnie and Clyde
we are forever tied.
From life to death
it's just her and I.

The Sun and Moon

When two magnetic energies fuse and become instantly synergistic. Few have experienced it, and to the outsiders it may seem mystic.

Supernova love, bound for explosive physics.

ECLIPSE

Rare as the darkest eclipse
in the night sky,
only a select few come across
a Sun or Moon
in their lives.

Together they elegantly align
the celestial silhouettes
of both body and mind.

Though it may seem to last
only for a short time,
rest assured knowing
the energy emitted and absorbed
will make waves for a lifetime.

Earthly Love

BLIND LOVE

If this love
ever turned out
to be blind...
I would elevate
all my other senses
just to find you again.

True beauty has never been one dimensional. Like a prism reflecting colors of light, beauty comes together from many facets such as appearance, personality, intellect, and ability to bond. Finding beauty across these layers creates a sustainable harmony that is irreplaceable.

BEAUTIFUL MIND

She's beautiful,
beautifully fine.
Her intellectual mind
has a beautiful design.
The type of book where
you read between the lines.
Cut past every grapevine
her love keeps me aligned
somewhere between her,
my desires and time.

Earthly Love

SYMBIOTICS

I show her
how to live,
I have never been
afraid of life.

She shows me
how to give,
she has always been
the angel type.

Magnetic puzzles
we move so swift
bound by the
chains of life.

Earthly Love

You will never find me wading ashore for you can catch me in the deep end.

I'll take my time to unravel every mental coil, leaving your world bent.

KEYS

Learning about herself
through me
she wonders how
I design my keys.
Removing every veil
she starts to become
afraid and pale
for every single
undiscovered place
I might reach.

Earthly Love

*When everything can be so right,
it seems so right, it feels so right,
yet there is that little void...
powerful enough to keep the destinies apart.*

LOST STAR

We're not so different
yet we are moving differently.

I love all of you,
you love the love inside of me.

I've found all of you,
you're still lost within the stars
you found in my first galaxy.

Perhaps one day we can
change pace, find our place,
against the love hurts fallacy.

Earthly Love

She never believed in love but love never believed in her beliefs. Now she knows otherwise, as open hearts sail the greatest of seas. This poetic card is for those scared of love, and how it will still find its place one way or another.

"Plate tectonics is a scientific theory that explains how major landforms are created as a result of Earth's subterranean movements. The theory, which solidified in the 1960s, transformed the earth sciences by explaining many phenomena, including mountain building events, volcanoes, and earthquakes."
- National Geographic (2023)

TECTONIC PLATES

She said she never
split her heart before
for somebody else.
I told her about
the tectonic plates
that came before
and how today's
world came about.
Lost in a gaze...
she still had doubts.
Until loves earthquake
paved her a way...
she finally figured it out.

Earthly Love

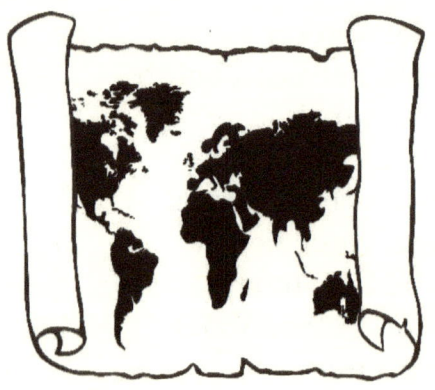

LANGUAGES

She's been around the world
culture flows inside her veins.
Still, she finds it insane
how my eyes...
speak so many languages
magnetically pulling her
out of her worldly frame.

Earthly Love

Love is by far one of the most mysterious concepts to capture. How do you define love? There are endless ways to go about it. Many philosophers, poets, writers and scientists have left their mark, yet none are universal. There is no right or wrong answer, except what makes YOU feel it.

This poetic card is my way of bringing love to the Deck of Poetry. May this resonate with some of you. One thing is for certain, love is what makes us human. It is by far the ultimate pursuit that brings us all together.

Love is but abundance.

LOVE

Love is the sensational
steep waterfall
that runs between
the wonder valleys
of one's heart
to one's mind.

Electric currents,
anti-gravity,
rippling feelings
beyond the mind's seal
one's steer conscious
cannot forever conceal.

Earthly Love

The power of a writer in love is their ability to immortalize it with words. As humans, we have an expiry date, yet our words are immortal.

This poetic card titled 'Lovetry' is a wordplay twist to poetry I created to describe a poet writing about love (pronounced like po-e-try / lov-e-try).

LOVETRY

I turn her
into poetry
only if her love
and vibrancy
deserves to be set
in words of stone.

Dancing in Ink

Part I

This poetic card is dedicated to all the creatives of the world: artists, writers, painters, teachers, philosophers, and counting.

MONSOONS

It's midnight,
I'm staring at the full moon.
My ink spills...in tune.
Inhale...my words of perfume
as I bloom and resume
in igniting off fumes.

On a creative thrill
I bring metamorphosis
to all my cocoons.
I rain down abundance
open up the floodgates
for my poetic monsoons.

An artist creates beauty which pulls on heartstrings and dances with the senses. Art is bending reality through imagination in which science cannot measure. Art births a symbiotic relationship among the art itself and the perception of the admirer. Regardless of what art form you embrace, you are bound by these timeless principles.

ARTIST

Forever addicted
to all that is creation.
I am a creator,
creating
creative creations
from the midst of thin air...
as if I am a magician
capable of fooling magic
or bringing hope to despair.

Know your soul, know your craft, and stay true to it all. The world will continue to change, in some ways for the better and others for the worse. The creativity inside us is our unique signature.

In this poetic card I express the power of creativity considering the Artificial Intelligence (AI) dilemma that has become so prominent today.

Killing two birds with one stone.

CREATIVITY

Creative since a fetus
with the mind power
of telekinesis.

Originality and soul
lingers inside my ink...
artificial intelligence
cannot form these pieces
or envision the thesis.

I lay down soil full of art
and watch how many seeds
in a lifetime it reaches,
while keeping it humble
like the very Earth
right beneath us.

Let your imagination roam free. Our ability to imagine as humans is truly profound, and incredibly important. It is responsible for many of our greatest inventions, ideas, or even creative joy.

This poetic card is an ode to the beauty of imagination and how I would express the depths of mine.

IMAGINATION

My mind wanders
from atoms
to distinct galaxies,
or predatory hunts
as the apex shark
deep down the oceans
to walking on top of
shallow seas.
My imagination
is always far beyond
just being open...
shapeshifting the fabric
of reality.

Dolphins are one of the rare few mammals that close one eye when they sleep; the left eye will be closed when the right half of the brain sleeps, and vice versa. This type of sleep is known as unihemispheric sleep as only one brain hemisphere sleeps at a time.

HYBRID

There is a nebula
inside my iris
as I paint pictures
inside both of my eyelids.

I sleep with one eye open,
a hybrid between
a dolphin and a pirate.

One eye stays open
to let the blue skies in.
The other stays closed
to explore galaxies within.

Haters will always hate, and that's fine. It's the approach in how you deal with this negativity that is most important. In essence, receiving "hate" can be a good sign! It indicates that you are onto something significant that holds enough merit to attract opposition.

Genuine dislike or constructive criticism aside, some "hate" because certain things you do forces others to reflect upon themselves. Haters have not accepted the roots of what really irks them inside.

No great artist has ever attained their title without someone hating it along the way. It is when they feel nothing at all that you should be most worried.

PHANTOM

Elusive phantom
to all the hatred,
I am touchless
for the basic.
They cannot fathom
the greatness
so they scavenge
and shape-shift.
The difference
between our souls is
only one's maskless.

The wolf is an animal that symbolizes freedom and spirit.

Life is finite and time continues to run, so make sure you and your gut instincts remain one.

WOLF

Visionary wolf...
alpha state of mind.
Unfazed by the sheep
inferior in design.

Witness my jaws
clench onto the world's neck
just so I can feel
my thoughts come alive.

Create the path that I seek,
I was never made for the hives.

Dancing in Ink

LABYRINTH

She tells me
she needs all of me,
yet I still get lost inside myself.

I'm navigating through a labyrinth
where the end just seems
to keep on vanishing.

I slay every single dragon within,
chasing enlightenment
of a higher-self over sin.

*Capturing the most guarded
of hearts oh-so swiftly.*

ROLLING STONE

Rolling stone alone
as I begin to roam
I can feel my own
inner-self emerging.

Inside her sacred dome
lies my geometric zone
symmetry...
I find myself submerging.

Bypassing the laws
of her guarded heart...
like a city's
well known surgeon.

The cities of the world are beautiful places and big ones truly have a life of their own. They exist outside the realm of day and night. My city is Toronto, Canada.

So many cities have passed historically and so many more will come to leave a mark. In this poetic card, I capture the essence of a big city in my signature poetry style.

THE CITY

The city never sleeps
as the matrix runs
far too deep.
From the lone wolves
to the flooded sheep
and everything else
that fits right in between;
it's a beautiful and damned scene.

Have you ever woken up and felt good with an abundance of energy? This poetic card entails that feeling.

I infused the Phoenix with the beauty of the Sun, which not only gives us life but also happiness. Rooted in Egyptian and Greek mythology, the Phoenix symbolizes immortality across cultures.

SUN RAYS

The sun shines daily.
Today I woke up
with deep intentions
to fully absorb it.

Carrying the rays
all within me,
I find metamorphosis.

Now a Golden Phoenix
dripped in flames of love,
I spread my wings across
to fly over our world
in hopes of restoring it.

Her name is Amazonia. Her love isn't for the weak.

AMAZONIA

Her heart is rich and complex
as if one's roaming around naked
in the Amazon jungle for context.
Careful to water the right flowers
and eat off all the right trees...
no poison is found in her streams
as the ecosystem stays clean.

Throughout the day and night
she's layered with intricacies
of sun blooms and nocturnal peace.
They say the best form of love
is both dangerous enough to kill
yet sweet enough to please.

Let me take you inside this fantasy world I created for my first Elfchen with the vision behind every line.

Line 1: Powerful kingdom with an Empress; ruling for many years.

Line 2: She is the most beautiful with a scent like none other.

Line 3: Do not be fooled, she is of regal blood and dangerous. Always ready for war or execution of betrayers.

Line 4: She is passionate, loving, and elegant, but in a way that is all consuming and empowering.

Line 5: This is how one ends up feeling on their own accord in her presence.

EMPRESS

Empress
Roses flowering
Regal thorns – sharpening
Her love dominates – devouring
Enslaved

Word-Smith & Play

Part II

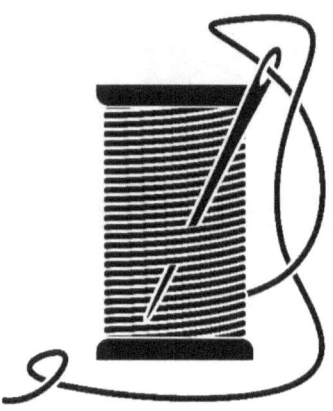

Just as the connoisseur is an expert judge in matters of taste, a poet is an expert judge in matters of capturing the human essence with words.

ARCHITECT

Elusive
architect of the mind...
may I pay hate no mind.
Spirituality elevated
by metaphysical pillars
is the poetry I design.
Every single thought
is well-tailored,
plus catered,
a connoisseur
for mankind.

If you have something that sparks your creativity, never bury it beneath everything else we deem important in life. The creative part of the mind is transcendental, putting you on an energetic wave that nothing else can reach.

PERFECTIONIST

Forget about your zodiac signs...
my wordplay represents
the right hemisphere.
Word perfectionist
come observe at this...
and you will find
no blemish here.

My thoughts
enter the matrix...
ink in blood is my fix.
Touching minds
is contagious...
I let it spill in many stages
and watch as poetry appears.

"Beneath the rule of men entirely great, the pen is mightier than the sword."

- Edward Bulwer-Lytton (1839)

SAMURAI

A samurai with
poetic confessions.
My sword slices
into your cerebral
and leaves behind
an emotional presence.

Your mind's shield
begins to fold
as I start to mold
into all five of your senses.
I simply assassinate...
with poetic blessings.

As a poet, I seek to create visuals and symbols that take your mind on a journey.

Every card in the Deck of Poetry can stand alone or be played together harmoniously.

If you have a talent of any kind, never shy away from embracing it. If you don't feel yourself, who will?

IMAGERY

Turn my words into pictures...
pictures into birds.
Flying above your scriptures
either I am gifted or cursed.

I sway your mind...
planting poetic seeds
for your soul to reap
with every single verse.

PICASSO

Picasso of words.
Vivid castles and swords.
Dark knights on a horse.

From peasants to lords,
I pleasantly pour...
poetry to both rich and poor.

Our greatest power is our ability to communicate. It is a common saying that actions speak louder than words, however, the power of precise articulation should never be underestimated.

WORDSMITH

Verbal assassin...
I load words as the bullets
and use this mind as a weapon.
Never do I require suppression.

I let my words sing loud and clear
penetrating the oppression.
Call me the Word-Smith & Wesson
shooting out poetic confessions.

Are you a creator? Does the power of the creative zone resonate with you? If so, what about that moment when all else fades away and you find yourself in a unique space of abundance, fluidity and magic? The power you manifest when in your creative element is one of the finest ways to nourish your soul's appetite.

POWER

Between the moment
I enter deep thoughts
that start to come alive
and every final word I inscribe
the world truly feels gripped inside...
the palm of my hands.

An ode to any artist, writer, poet, innovator, or speaker that is never afraid to challenge the status quo and question motives.

DRAGON SLAYER

Call me the Dragon Slayer.
I've come to free minds
from societal chains,
never prescribed in prayers.

Linguistic sword in hand,
for every forsaken beast
inside the dungeon I land
precision strikes inked
by my poetic hands...
liberating forgotten souls
from societal quicksand.

Haiku Den

Part III

Haiku Den

LIGHT

The dark sky anchors...
yet the ship of light can't drown.
It rights every left.

Haiku Den

Mastering the execution of every poem and observing how it transcends onto others' heartstrings is the poet's mission.

POET'S DREAM

Quill spills poetry.
Paint words, touch souls gracefully.
Pull strings - poet's dream.

Haiku Den

Artists offer so much of their lives to bring color to humanity. Whether we look back throughout history or all the unique ways of today, art has been a pillar of what makes us human and leaves timeless relics behind.

MARTYR

Earth, Fire, Water.
Tsunami inside my pen
spills life, art's martyr.

Deck of Poetry: The Wolf's Ink

WOLF'S INK

Wolf and the night sky.
Moon howls echo me alive.
Ink inside my eyes.

THE END

Thank you for being a part of this journey and reading my debut poetry book.

Words cannot describe my gratitude.

Follow me on Instagram *@deckofpoetry*

Visit *www.deckofpoetry.com*

www.ingramcontent.com/pod-product-compliance
Lightning Source LLC
Chambersburg PA
CBHW031108080526
44587CB00011B/883